Seattle SuperSonics

Michael E. Goodman

CREATIVE EDUCATION

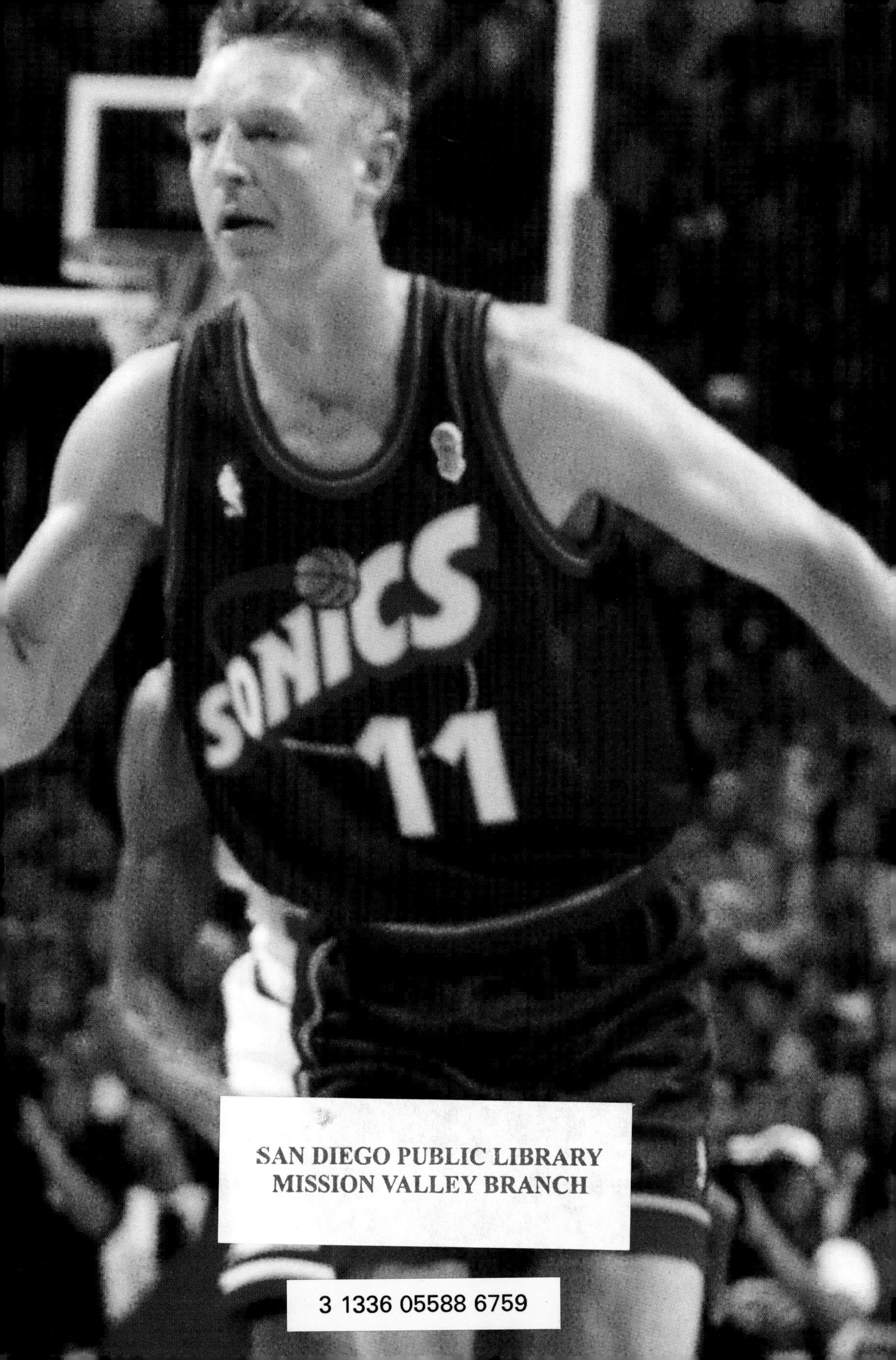
SONICS
11

Published by Creative Education
123 South Broad Street, Mankato, Minnesota 56001
Creative Education is an imprint of The Creative Company

Designed by Rita Marshall

Photos by: Allsport Photography, Associated Press/Wide World Photos,
Focus on Sports, NBA Photos, UPI/Corbis-Bettmann, and SportsChrome.

Photo page 1: Terry Cummings
Photo title page: Detlef Schrempf

Library of Congress Cataloging-in-Publication Data

Goodman, Michael E.
Seattle SuperSonics / Michael E. Goodman.
p. cm. — (NBA today)
Summary: Describes the background and history of the Seattle SuperSonics
pro basketball team.
ISBN 0-88682-891-0

1. Seattle SuperSonics (Basketball team)—Juvenile literature.
[1. Seattle SuperSonics (Basketball team)—History. 2. Basketball—History.]
I. Title. II. Series: NBA today (Mankato, Minn.)

GV885.52.S4G66 1997   96-52963
796.323'64'09797772—dc21

No other city in the United States blends man-made and natural elements more gracefully than does Seattle, Washington. The city's urban skyline, featuring the famous 607-foot-high Space Needle, is recognizable to people all over the world. Yet the Space Needle and the other man-made structures of Seattle are dwarfed by the majestic presence of snowcapped Mount Rainier rising in the distance. And the gold, red, and brown colors of the city's buildings fit comfortably with the surrounding green forests and the clear blue waters of Puget Sound.

While the residents of Seattle are justifiably proud of their

All-time Sonics great Lenny Wilkens.

Seattle's first-ever draft pick Al Tucker was named to the NBA All-Rookie team.

city's natural beauty, they also like to emphasize the city's role as a major industrial center—particularly its importance as the world's largest manufacturer of jet aircraft. That was one reason why, when it came time to pick a name for Seattle's franchise in the National Basketball Association (NBA) in 1966, the choice was the SuperSonics.

For more than 30 years, the SuperSonics have lived up to their name, featuring fast-moving and high-flying teams that have earned respect throughout the league. Many unique talents have performed in Seattle over the years, including Spencer Haywood, Lenny Wilkens, Slick Watts, Fred Brown, Dennis Johnson, Jack Sikma, Tom Chambers, Dale Ellis, and Xavier McDaniel. Yet the club has not been known as much for its superstars as for its excellent balance and teamwork. The current Sonics, with Shawn Kemp, Detlef Schrempf, and Gary Payton, are carrying on that tradition as they strive together to reach the upper levels of the NBA.

WILKENS EARNS AND BUILDS RESPECT

The Sonics started their history far from the top of the NBA. In fact, the team completed its first season, 1967–68, with the second-worst record in the league. But that type of finish was to be expected from an expansion club whose roster was composed mostly of aging veterans and raw rookies.

"Sometimes we were fueled by fear and hope more than anything else," recalled Al Bianchi, who was head coach during the Sonics' first two seasons. "Our guys hadn't even had a chance to get to know each other. But there we were

NBA Defensive Player of the Year Gary Payton.

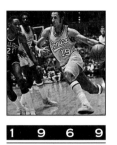

*Lenny Wilkens's
1,835 points and
22.4 average were
the highest marks
of his career.*

heading into Boston Garden, the Forum, or the Spectrum to take on the Bill Russells, Elgin Baylors, and Wilt Chamberlains. It was a little intimidating, but our attitude was, 'Okay, we've got a chance to play against the best in the world, so let's go out and beat the best in the world.' "

One of Seattle's biggest problems during its initial season was that it lacked leadership. All of that changed before the 1968–69 campaign when the Sonics traded top scorer Walt Hazzard to the St. Louis Hawks for All-Star guard Lenny Wilkens. An excellent passer and shooter, Wilkens brought savvy and experience to the Seattle lineup. Not only did he produce fine individual statistics in 1968–69, ranking second in the league in assists and ninth in scoring, but he also provided clearer direction for both the offense and defense. With Wilkens as quarterback, the club produced seven more victories than in the previous year. Nevertheless, the two losing seasons were just too much for coach Bianchi. He made the decision to resign.

Seattle general manager Dick Vertlieb wasted no time picking Bianchi's replacement. He offered the job to Lenny Wilkens, who agreed to serve as player/coach for only one year "just in case things don't work out." But things worked out well, and Wilkens went on to serve for three successful seasons in his dual role.

As a player, Wilkens had always understood the importance of teamwork and mutual respect in basketball. When he became a player/coach, he fostered that same understanding among his team members. "There is nothing like respect on a basketball team—toward the coach, toward one another," he said. "And I tried to set an example. My players knew that I would give up the ball, that I would pass. That made it easier for them to do the same."

Little by little, under Wilkens's direction, the Sonics began to win consistently. But sometimes the player/coach had to take drastic action to remind the players that they had to work together as a unit. One night in 1970, for example, he fined every member of the Sonics—including himself—$100 following a close loss to the Detroit Pistons. "Some of the guys had broken elementary rules of training," he explained. "I fined the innocent with the guilty. Basketball is so much a team game, I wanted the innocent ones to ride the guilty."

During Wilkens's third year at the helm, the SuperSonics produced their first winning record, 47–35, and came close to making the playoffs. Wilkens wasn't the only reason for the club's success; another was the presence of young scoring sensation Spencer Haywood, whom team owner Sam Schulman had wooed away from Denver in the American Basketball Association (ABA). The 22-year-old Haywood finished second in the league in scoring, was among the leaders in rebounding, and was named to the All-NBA squad.

"When Spencer was on, he could demoralize the other team single-handedly," said Sonics center Bob Rule. "He'd pull up from 25 feet and launch one after another into the rafters. Somehow the ball would usually come down snap in the center of the basket."

Despite Haywood's heroics and the club's increasing success, Lenny Wilkens decided to give up his role as coach following the 1971–72 season. He was soon shocked to find out that he would no longer be playing in Seattle, either. The Sonics traded their first great leader to Cleveland for young

1 9 7 0

Bob Rule topped the Sonics in both scoring and rebounding for the second straight year.

Spencer Haywood, a legendary star.

Like Haywood, Jack Sikma was a standout.

guard Butch Beard. Sonics fans were sad to see Wilkens leave, but he would be back.

Dick Snyder was among the league's top free-throw shooters, ranking seventh in the NBA.

ENTER BIG BILL RUSSELL AND TINY SLICK WATTS

When Lenny Wilkens left Seattle, he took with him some of the pride and cohesiveness that had characterized the team during his years with the club. The 1972–73 season was a disaster, as the Sonics' record plummeted to 26–56. Owner Sam Schulman knew that something dramatic had to be done to turn the team around. He decided to hire Bill Russell, often called the greatest player in NBA history, to coach the club. Russell had led the Boston Celtics to nine championships in 10 years as a player and two titles in three years as a player/coach.

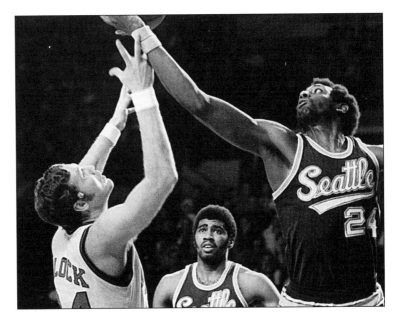

Scoring sensation Spencer Haywood.

Russell knew how to win, but he didn't always take the best approach in coaching others to win. He felt that every player on his team should be as talented and committed to winning as he had been when he was a player. During Russell's four years as coach in Seattle, his demanding nature and lack of patience often created a feeling of uneasiness between players and management.

Yet the Sonics improved dramatically under Russell's stern control. Within two years of Russell's arrival in Seattle, the Sonics were back on the winning track, producing a 43–39 record in 1974–75 and earning their first playoff berth.

The club's offensive leaders during that campaign were Spencer Haywood and guard Fred Brown, whose long-range bombs earned him the nickname "Downtown Freddy Brown." They made a terrific inside/outside tandem, with each averaging more than 21 points per game during the year. Brown would go on to play 13 seasons with the Sonics, mostly as the team's sixth man supreme, and he remains the club's all-time scoring leader.

Another player who emerged as a star under Russell's leadership was Donald Earl Watts, better known to fans as "Slick." Watts was a unique person on and off the court. At 5-foot-11 and 165 pounds, he was one of the smallest players in the NBA, yet he made a place for himself with his speed and desire. Slick had two trademarks: one was the bright green headband he wore on his shiny bald head during games and the other was the lightning-quick hands that enabled him to steal the basketball from opponents.

Watts became a great favorite in Seattle, not only for his style of play, but also for his kindness and generosity off the

1 9 7 4

Bill Russell's Sonics hosted their first NBA All-Star Game on January 15.

court. Between games and during the off-season, he crammed his schedule with surprise playground visits, free high school clinics, and trips to children's wards at various local hospitals.

"I always tell kids to think how they'd like to be treated, and then to do the same to others," Slick explained. "And one more thing: Believe in yourself. If you believe you can do something, don't let anybody in the whole world tell you that you can't."

Watts put his own advice to the test when he first came to Seattle in 1973 as a little-known free agent out of Xavier University in Louisiana. Watts's hustle and talent earned him a spot on the Sonics' roster that year, but not a place in the lineup. He rode the bench for the first 30 games of the season and only got onto the court during the closing seconds of blowouts. Meanwhile, Seattle fans were beginning to chant, "We want Slick. We want Slick."

"We were losing, and the fans didn't have anything else to cheer for," Watts recalled. "I remember Russ [Russell] put me in against Portland and I hit a fade-away falling out of bounds. I got my confidence from that one shot. A few days later, Russ started me against Atlanta and Pistol Pete Maravich and said, 'I'm tired of this no-pass, no-teamwork team.' I blocked three of Pistol's shots, got 21 points, nine rebounds, and 14 assists. I was doing things Jerry West and Dave Bing did, not some guy named Slick."

After that game in Atlanta, Watts became one of the keys to the Sonics' offense and defense, and for the next several years, he never stopped hustling and he continued to return the fans' affection.

Seattle folk hero Slick Watts.

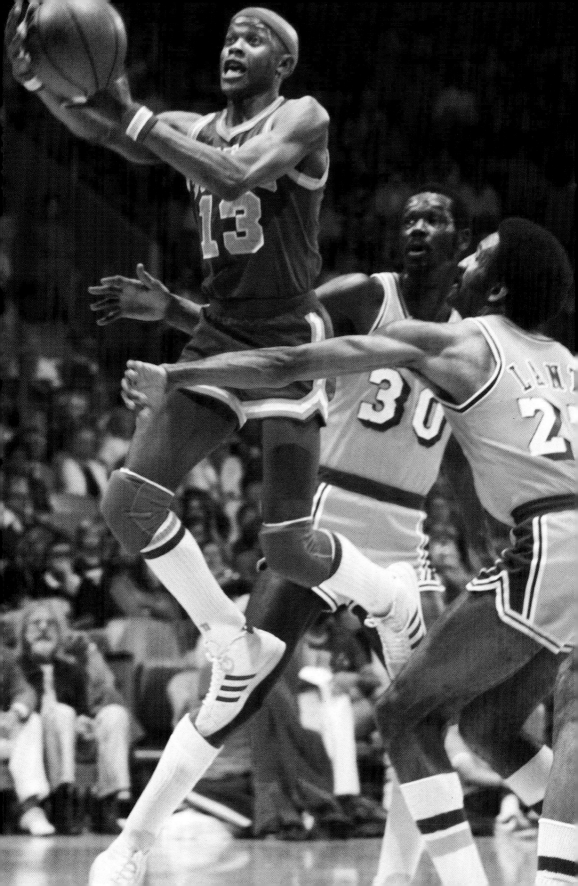

Slick Watts became the first Sonics player named to the NBA's All-Defensive team.

When Sam Schulman was asked in 1976 if he had a favorite all-time Sonic, he replied, "In the 10 years of the Sonics, I don't know of one player on a par with Slick Watts as far as desire on the court and ability to make people happy. That's a fact. I wish I had 12 Slick Wattses on my team."

By the 1976–77 season, conditions had changed greatly in Seattle—for the worse. Players were traded or benched with little explanation. Spencer Haywood, who had often had trouble getting along with coach Russell, had been sent to the New York Knicks the year before and took his offensive weapons with him. Rookie guards Dennis Johnson and Bob Wilkerson were taking playing time away from Slick Watts and Fred Brown, which the two veterans resented. Other fan favorites were also sent packing or kept on the bench. Finally, the Seattle fans and players had had more than enough of Bill Russell's dictatorial methods. They began demanding that the coach be replaced. Sam Schulman gave in to the demands, and Russell was forced to resign at the end of the season. It was the end of one important era in the history of the SuperSonics, but just the beginning of an even more exciting time.

WILKENS'S RETURN KEYS SONICS' SUCCESS STORY

Bill Russell's departure looked like a terrible mistake during the first month of the 1977–78 season. Russell's replacement, Bob Hopkins, a former NBA player and Sonics assistant, had a lot of trouble getting the players' attention and respect. One-fourth of the way through the season, the Sonics were mired in last place in their division with a 5–17 record. So Sam Schulman decided to make another quick change. He turned to the club's new general manager—an old friend named Lenny Wilkens—and asked him to take over once again as coach.

For several of the Sonics who had resented Hopkins even more than Russell, the coaching change was a reason for optimism. "I've got to say that being with Lenny is like getting out of jail," said one Seattle player. Wilkens made some immediate personnel changes. He converted Fred Brown from a starter to sixth man, relying on his firepower off the bench to provide a quick lift to the Sonics' attack. Newly acquired Gus Williams took Brown's place as a starter and responded by leading the team in scoring. Wilkens also moved another new acquisition, Marvin Webster, to the starting center position and shifted rookie Jack Sikma to power forward. The 7-foot-2 Webster, whose nickname was "the Human Eraser" because of his shot-blocking skills, responded by becoming an offensive as well as defensive force. Meanwhile, Sikma became a devastating outside shooter and top rebounder from the wing. In addition, young point guard Dennis Johnson began to assert himself as the team's floor general and as an outstanding defender. Johnson's play thrilled everyone except Slick Watts, who demanded a trade when he lost his starting position.

Wilkens's "new" Sonics began to win . . . and win . . . and win some more. The team went 42–18 over the last three-fourths of the year and roared into the playoffs. "What did Wilkens have that Russell and Hopkins lacked?" asked Seattle sportswriter Blaine Johnson. "Maybe more organization, maybe more communication, maybe he wound up with the

Long-distance shooter Fred Brown topped all Seattle scorers for the second season in a row.

Seattle rose to the top in the mid-1970s (pages 18–19).

*Power forward Jack
Sikma earned a
berth on the league
All-Rookie team.*

right blend of personalities. One thing is certain, he put all the necessary ingredients into the pot at the right time." The Sonics continued their winning ways in the playoffs, racing past the Los Angeles Lakers, then the defending champion Portland Trail Blazers, and finally the Denver Nuggets to reach the NBA finals. There, they faced off against the young and hungry Washington Bullets, led by Wes Unseld and Elvin Hayes.

It was a classic confrontation. At first, Seattle seemed destined to wear the NBA crown. The Sonics captured game one at home by roaring back from a 19-point deficit in the final 14 minutes to gain a 106–102 victory. The teams split the next four games, and Seattle needed just one more win for the title. Then things fell apart for the Sonics. Washington destroyed Seattle in game six by 35 points—an NBA finals record—to even the series, and then survived a desperate Sonics comeback in the closing minutes of game seven to win the championship.

The Sonics' players and fans vowed they would be back the next year. And they were. In fact, the same two teams squared off in the 1979 NBA finals. The Sonics weren't exactly the same, however, as Lenny Wilkens had made some more lineup changes. Marvin Webster had been lost to the New York Knicks as a free agent, so Wilkens shifted Jack Sikma back into the pivot, where his speed, shooting touch, and driving ability helped him outmaneuver most opposing centers. The forwards were Lonnie Shelton, the team's enforcer, who had come to Seattle from New York as compensation for the signing of Webster, and silky smooth John Johnson. Gus Williams and Dennis Johnson remained at guard, forming one of the finest backcourt tandems in the league. And Fred Brown and Paul Silas provided instant offense and leadership off the bench. Together, these players formed the "Seattle Seven," and they were unstoppable in the NBA finals. The Sonics devastated the defending champion Bullets four games to one, bringing Seattle an NBA championship banner.

REBUILDING IN THE 1980s

Unfortunately, the Sonics were unable to carry the magic of those two seasons into the early 1980s. One reason was the acquisition of superstar Magic Johnson by the Sonics' rival, the Los Angeles Lakers. Johnson helped turn the Lakers into perennial Pacific Division and Western Conference champions. Meanwhile, the Sonics lost much of their nucleus during the next few years, the result of trades, retirements, and contract disputes. Within three years, the only members of the "Seattle Seven" who remained in the Pacific Northwest were Jack Sikma, Fred Brown, and Gus Williams.

Thanks largely to Sikma's consistent play, the Sonics continued to record winning seasons, although they could never progress past the second round of the playoffs. Sikma spent nine seasons with the SuperSonics before asking to be traded following the 1985–86 season. He played in more than 700 games for Seattle. Despite his lean frame, he was an outstanding rebounder and shot-blocker. He ranks as the team's career leader in rebounds and second in blocked shots. He also ranks second in total points scored.

By the time Sikma left the Sonics, a new coach and a few

1 9 7 9

To cap off the championship year, Dennis Johnson was named MVP of the NBA finals.

Fred Brown, a member of the "Seattle Seven."

new stars were on the scene in Seattle. The coach was long-time Bullets assistant Bernie Bickerstaff, who replaced Lenny Wilkens before the 1985–86 season. Bickerstaff's job was to revitalize a Sonics team that had lost much of its enthusiasm on the court.

"Bernie has a way of communicating with the players that makes us want to listen," said guard Danny Young. "He basically won't let us get down on ourselves."

Bickerstaff and the Sonics suffered through a rocky year in 1985–86, finishing with a 31–51 record, but two young stars spent the season honing their skills. They were forwards Xavier McDaniel and Tom Chambers. McDaniel, the club's first-round draft choice out of Wichita State, barely lost out to New York's Patrick Ewing as NBA Rookie of the Year in 1985–86. He posted more than 600 rebounds and averaged 17 points a game. The fans began calling him the "X-Man," as in "X-cellent." Chambers, at 6-foot-10, had the size to play power forward and the speed and moves to be a small forward. He led the team in scoring and in spectacular dunks.

Going into the 1986–87 season with an experienced frontcourt composed of Sikma, McDaniel, and Chambers, Bernie Bickerstaff was confident of his team's ability to regain its winning form. The club also made key changes in the backcourt, drafting Nate McMillan out of North Carolina State and making a trade with Dallas for three-point shooting wizard Dale Ellis.

It took awhile for the players to blend into a cohesive unit, but they were peaking by playoff time. Having recorded only the seventh-best record in the West during the regular season (39–43), Seattle was a decided underdog

Gus Williams, who led the Sonics in scoring, assists, and steals, was named to the All-NBA team.

23

1 9 8 7

All-Star Game MVP Tom Chambers scored 34 points in 29 minutes, leading to a 154– 149 overtime win.

against the second-seeded Dallas Mavericks in the first round—particularly since the Mavs had swept all five games against Seattle during the season. But Dale Ellis was out for revenge against his former teammates, and he keyed the Sonics to a speedy three-games-to-one victory.

In the conference semifinals, Ellis, Chambers, and Mc-Daniel remained hot, and the Sonics romped over Houston. All Seattle had to do was get by its old rivals, the Los Angeles Lakers, and it would earn a berth in the NBA finals. Suddenly the club's magic ended, however, and the Lakers eliminated the Sonics in four straight games. But it had been an exciting run while it lasted.

"We played clean but mean," said McDaniel. "We had something to prove and nothing to lose. So we went out there like warriors and surprised everybody."

Hopes were high in Seattle for the next season, particularly with the addition of 6-foot-10 rookie forward Derrick McKey to the team. The incredibly versatile McKey quickly established himself as the team's sixth man. At one time or another during his rookie season, he played all five positions on the court.

"McKey has many gifts," said NBA analyst and former star Rick Barry. "He can drill the three-pointer or be on the receiving end of an alley-oop; he can put it on the floor with either hand and tomahawk-dunk the finish, or he can hurt you with his turnaround jumper. He's also capable of flat-out shutting down his man on defense."

McKey's presence helped the Sonics improve their record to 44–38 in 1987–88, but they were quickly eliminated in the playoffs. The team's brain trust of Bernie Bickerstaff and general manager K.C. Jones decided to continue the rebuilding process.

First, the Sonics declined to match an offer made by Phoenix to free agent Tom Chambers, so the high-scoring forward packed his bags and left. Then, to replace Chambers, Seattle obtained Michael Cage in a trade with the Los Angeles Clippers. A powerful rebounder, especially on the offensive boards, Cage provided new strength for the Super-Sonic attack. His ability to play both center and power forward also added to the Sonics' flexibility.

With Cage and Olden Polynice alternating at center, Ellis and Nate McMillan at guard, and McKey and McDaniel at forward, the Sonics had another fine season in 1988–89 (47–35), but failed once again in the playoffs. That didn't sit well with the team's management or fans. And when the club didn't even qualify for the playoffs the following year, it was clear that more changes were needed.

1 9 8 9

Dale Ellis set a team one-season scoring record with 2,253 points.

BUILDING A TEAM FOR THE '90S

Starting with K.C. Jones's moving from the front office to the sidelines as head coach, and continuing with the melding of guards Gary Payton and teenage sensation Shawn Kemp into the lineup, the Sonics revamped again for the new decade. But for some club veterans, the changes just created an uneasy feeling. "I'm sure used to the turnover by now," said Xavier McDaniel. "But somewhere along the line you wonder when it will stop. When will the team stay together and have a chance to grow?"

McDaniel never received the answer to his question. He

The incredible Detlef Schrempf (pages 26–27).

With a 92 percent average, Ricky Pierce ranked third in the NBA in free-throw shooting.

too was traded away, going to Phoenix early in the 1990–91 season. Then, halfway through the 1991–92 season, the club replaced coach K.C. Jones with George Karl.

Karl had a reputation as a genius with a big ego. He had been a player in San Antonio and had coached for both Cleveland and Golden State. But NBA teams eventually had enough of his ego, and Karl was forced to take jobs in the Continental Basketball Association and in Europe before being hired by Seattle. The decision to hire Karl turned out to be the right one, as Karl got the most out of his two potential young superstars—guard Gary Payton and forward Shawn Kemp.

"He's a stud in every game," said Karl of Payton. "He does what we need, and his consistency in that area is why he has to be considered an MVP candidate."

K.C. Jones remembers when he first saw Shawn Kemp play high school ball on videotape. "I saw this kid with such enthusiasm for rebounding and blocking shots. That really impressed me—a high school kid who had that."

On the back of 22-year-old Kemp's scoring and rebounding prowess, Karl's Sonics finished with the best record in the NBA's regular season in 1993–94. The duo emerged as one of the best combinations in the NBA—Shawn Kemp made the All-NBA second team, and Payton was named to the NBA All-Defensive first team.

"We decided to give up our summer vacations," said Kemp. "We went to the gyms. Man, we worked."

"They've always been the two young guys," said Karl of his duo. "Now they've blossomed into perennial All-Stars."

"We've always wanted to create our own style, our own

names," said Kemp. "We've put the time in and made the guys around us better, and we've talked about finishing our careers together."

Kemp and Payton were graced with such talented teammates as Detlef Schrempf and Sam Perkins. Schrempf, a high-scoring forward and native of Germany, proved to be not only one of the NBA's most accurate shooters, but also one of the Sonics' leaders in assists and rebounds. Sam Perkins, who played with NBA stars Michael Jordan and James Worthy on an NCAA champion North Carolina squad, proved to be a great outside shooter and inside rebounder.

Despite fielding what was one of the most talented teams in the NBA, the Sonics were unable to find the chemistry needed to win it all. They continued to be one of the top teams in the league, but always came up against a stronger

1 9 9 6

Veteran guard Hersey Hawkins topped the 100 steal mark for the eighth straight season.

Three-point shooter Sam Perkins.

Shawn Kemp, "The Reign Man."

Hersey Hawkins, an enduring star.

31

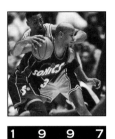

Terry Cummings, a midseason acquisition, played in his 90th career playoff game.

foe in the playoffs. This was clearest in 1995–96 when the SuperSonics powered their way to a 64–18 record, only to face the 72–10 Chicago Bulls in the NBA finals. While Chicago won the series in six games, the Sonics proved they were contenders, winning back-to-back games against the powerhouse Bulls.

In 1997—with the assistance of Jim McIlvaine and veterans Hersey Hawkins and Terry Cummings—Payton's 21 points per game solidified an up-and-down 57-25 season. Despite a lengthy late-season slump by Shawn Kemp, the Sonics defended their Pacific Division championship. Though Kemp was back to his old form in the playoffs, his efforts weren't enough to push Seattle over the top of Charles Barkley and a veteran Houston club. The Houston series was a tough seven-game battle, but the loss shouldn't dampen the spirits of Sonics fans. Payton and Kemp have many good years ahead of them and they're ready to shoot for the stars again. The right chemistry to pull off a future Seattle championship appears to be firmly in place—all fans have to do is watch and wait.

T